Animals & ABCs

Arty Imaginarium's Worlds of Diversity

AuthorHouse™
1663 Liberty Drive
Bloomington, IN 47403
www.authorhouse.com
Phone: 833-262-8899

The views expressed in this work are solely those of the author and do not necessarily reflect the views of the publisher, and the publisher hereby disclaims any responsibility for them.

This book is printed on acid-free paper.

ISBN: 979-8-8230-0160-1 (sc)
ISBN: 979-8-8230-0161-8 (hc)
ISBN: 979-8-8230-0159-5 (e)

Library of Congress Control Number: 2023903339

Print information available on the last page.

Published by AuthorHouse 04/21/2023

authorHOUSE

For my Oak tree.

– Love, Mom

A is for ape.

Ardin the ape is amazed; he is reading about a boy.

B is for boy.

Brandi the boy is writing a book about a cat.

C is for cat.

Charley the cat is creating a ditty about a dog.

D is for dog.

Dori the dog is daydreaming about being an elephant.

E is for elephant.

Eli the elephant is excited to meditate like a fox.

F is for fox.

Fredly the fox is having a fabulous dream about a girl.

 is for girl.

A girl named Golden is giggling with the happy hare.

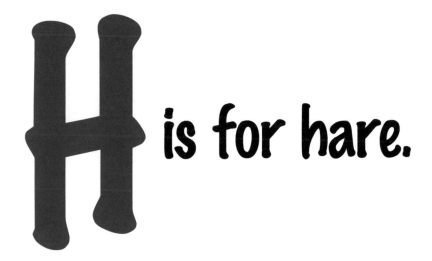 is for hare.

Hero the hare is sharing an instant message with an inchworm.

I is for inchworm.

Izzy the inchworm
is writing a letter
to a jaguar.

J is for jaguar.

Jira the jaguar
is learning what
kangaroos do.

K is for kangaroo.

Kami the kangaroo
is writing lyrics
for a llama.

L is for llama.

Lou the llama is playing music for little Miss Mouse.

M is for mouse.

Maki the mouse
is playing the
flute for a newt.

N is for newt.

Nyx the newt is neatly writing a paper for an owl.

O is for owl.

Ollie the owl is opening a letter from a panda.

P is for panda.

Parker the panda is preparing a meal to share with a quail.

Q is for quail.

Queeny the quail is asking a rat a question.

R is for rat.

A rat named Ranger is reading a recipe from a squirrel.

S is for squirrel.

Sunny the squirrel is shy but wants to tutor a turtle.

T is for turtle.

Tetris the turtle is telling everyone about his friend the unicorn.

U is for unicorn.

Uma the unicorn is unwrapping a present from a vulture.

V is for vulture.

Vinny the vulture
is venturing out
to find a walrus.

W is for walrus.

Willie the walrus is whispering a bedtime story to a xeme.

 is for xeme.

Xara the xeme is sketching a picture for a yeti.

Y is for yeti.

Yogi the yeti is teaching a zebra to yodel.

Z is for zebra.

Zemi the zebra
is zipping around,
delivering this
book ... to you!

Printed in the United States
by Baker & Taylor Publisher Services